CORMORANT

Elisa Carlsen

Attention schools and businesses: for discounted copies on bulk
orders, please contact the publisher directly. Booksellers can
order copies from Ingram.

For information contact:
Unsolicited Press
Portland, Oregon
www.unsolicitedpress.com
orders@unsolicitedpress.com
619-354-8005

Cover Design: Kathryn Gerhardt
Cover Artwork: Elisa Carlsen
Editor: Summer Stewart

ISBN: 978-1-956692-67-9

The poems in this collection were inspired by my time working on the Cormorant Project[1] and are dedicated to the memory of Sharnelle Fee, Founder of the Wildlife Center of the North Coast.

---

[1] A federal project which killed thousands of double-crested cormorants to reduce their consumption of threatened and endangered juvenile salmon and steelhead in the Columbia River Estuary.

POEMS

INTERSTITIAL SPACE 1

SCIENTIFIC INTEGRITY 3

PROSPECTING 5

FORAGER 7

SOCIAL ATTRACTION 8

NEST INITIATION 10

HATCHED 11

CLUTCH 12

FLEDGLING 14

HUMAN DIMENSIONS 15

TAXONOMY 17

COLONY 18

MIGRATION 20

THREATENED AND ENDANGERED 21

ORDER OF MAGNITUDE 22

BANDED 23

PEER REVIEW 25

DETERMINISTIC BEHAVIOR 26

FEATHERS 27

SUMMARY JUDGMENT 28

GOONEY BIRD 29

CORMORANT

INTERSTITIAL SPACE

you were always more bird than body of Christ,
ranging far above the blue-gray pulse of water,

above the emerald fields of your favorite river valley
most alive on foggy mornings

where the only light of day comes late
but fits the mood-like mystic.

and where you left us for the salted waves,
and secret lives of gulls.

I came here only because I hoped to find
something of myself / or other missing things,

but I had no point of bearing to the true West,
and I got lost along its hallowed edge.

to live / I had to learn / to take
my rain like medicine
until it blended with my blood
and thinned me out so I could float

past our storied river's bar,
where the shipwrecks and seiners
lost their songs to the sea.

past the shoals and coastal cliffs,

to all the water in the world…

SCIENTIFIC INTEGRITY

there is no doubt you went
between the folds
of interstitial space
in deterministic beat.

I bet you measure
the many moods of waterbirds
behind a perfect blind,
with your still, empirical heart.

and even though it's been years
since your last sighting,
there are echoes of you here...

a lasting, long-winded coo
roosting in the snags
of second-growth Sitka

from the sandy, yellow shore,
where a cormorant, double-crested,
dives in the air.

and where someone,
who has loved something sacred
gives it back to its wild,
like you / were given to yours.

PROSPECTING

the steel bridge rises in government green.
a heavy metal mountain
over the Columbia.
over the ocean's tidal reach.
over Mary Todd's in Uniontown
and a fleet of fishing boats
waiting out the weather in port.

on quartered cloverleaf, I ascend
its piers packed with dark, gangly birds
with bright blue, fluorescent eyes.
I see them gauging the speed of the wind,
and the probable depth of their prey.

I feel so lonely watching them,
heading out over the choppy, cold water

they have no choice / but to dive.

I, on the other hand,
looked a log time into the mirror
at a life, I measured poorly and shortchanged,

and said, "yes,
I will fill my pockets with complicated grief.
I will break my bones to sit in a cage."

FORAGER

my mouth is desperate and acts alone.
I spend years catching up to it.
by then / you have gone.
now,
I begin every sentence
with sorry.

you went somewhere I can't go,
stitched in the sound wave of birdsong.
a haunting, perfect pitch
drifting softly in the low ceiling of storm clouds
that reminds me of,
what it was I should have left alone
but didn't.

and my belly is full of the reasons why.
and they all start with someone else's name.

SOCIAL ATTRACTION

I wonder about you,
my maybe friend
with your tin-tin heart,
a wolf trap for misfits
and their kin.

you love wild things so much,
the fingers on your hand
blur into a web,
and look like pelican feet
standing one-legged on driftwood.

your bright brown /sea lion eyes
shining, ever watching
that great blue bear,
the ocean.

your raspy voice,
sounding like a DOS printer,
running out of time,
until it did.

if I could wish you back,
with my dark birdy poems

just for the few sunny days
we get here,
I would.

NEST INITIATION

every beginning
is a particle of light
exploding into the sun
expanding uniformly,
until we appear to shoulder
the wonder of it all.
carve our story from time,
and make count
the exact number of days
we have to be here.

because when they pass
we'll call back to them.
heads full of nostalgia,
for the dive bars and hullabaloo crowds,
for our weird and hungry hearts,
still longing to be filled,

like a river / waiting for rain
like I / was waiting for you.

HATCHED

some birds, like us
are born featherless,
mouths open, hungry for it all,
shameless with a need
that makes it hard to live
and harder still to love.

somehow, we survive it,
perfect circles among many squares,
alone in a world that fits us
like other people's clothes.
we get along
with cigarettes and long nights,

and me dreaming you
and you dreaming me,
into the blue-gray curve
of an indelicate world,
that deepens if only
for the seconds we were in it.

CLUTCH

even though we came here
from the same nowhere before,
rose up / in a similar brood
and drank from the same river
of lost shoes and dirty fish,

we don't look like each other at all.

my heart turned rueful
and talked too much
and you were the candle
I could have been

if,

the lives that separated us
hadn't stretched me out
in long stares
over bodies
over buildings
sounding the distance.

if,

the distance itself
hadn't become my calling.

FLEDGLING

all my life / I've tried to slip the knot,
tied to the bow of my body from birth.
wanted to lift my life up
and conform the shape of me
to something the world could love.

instead, I entered every room
awkward and unordained.
stuck in that space between space,
where lost things live.
who only want to feel
the promise of their life again.

like a pursuit-diver / on a broken piling,
near the mix of salt and cold, dark water.
who dives to break a transverse wave
down to unfathomable depths.
in the singular purpose of their skill
and the orbit of their own time.

HUMAN DIMENSIONS

stern-faced and beautiful
you set your life to sail
like a butterfly boat
ported from the city
crowded with desire
going your way
until I got on mine.

and we crossed under
that ever-gray, Astorian sky.

where you / divided me.

I could tell you were tired
from everything,
all the time, everything
but still, you leaned into me,
as if to say…

I hope someday
something wakes up inside of you

tenders your darkness,
catches your fall

and turns you back to water.

TAXONOMY

among noble,
water-colored kinds of birds
I am unspecialized,

singular, with sad tones
a blue-blazing, wistful scavenger.

I excel in the distance,
the push-offs and empty sets,
where I see something
not quite there.

like you and I laughing
coming back to shore
from our lost, longing years.

to be in the same room
on the same side.

the salt / still stinging our eyes

after all that rain.

COLONY

set flush against a cold spring rain,
after a long time behind the blind,
the first sighting - a spec,
the last - a blur.

a matte black, shimmering wave
of iridescent feathers and shit.
as twenty thousand cormorants
step over each other

necks bent in spring affection.
gular pouches in Sunkist orange
their crested tufts hanging
like a laurel-leaf Roman crown.

their smell is still with me.
a mix of rotten fish, and sulfur
that steals the breath from my lungs.

I watch a mated pair toss the body
of a young, dead bird
back and forth, up in the air and

catch it in their beaks.

I take notes and tally the score.

MIGRATION

it is not so much a river anymore,
it is machine-forged now.
a mass of damned steel and rubble,
slowed down the whole way
by a need that will never go
until we do.

in government-speak, it is called:
Federal Columbia River Power System,
or Columbia River System Operations,
depending on the lawsuit
and who is in charge of public affairs.

translated, it means a bunch of dams.
run of river or high head,
built with rebar
broken treaties
and big rocks.

to keep air / entrained in water.

home to wild fish,
just barely.

THREATENED AND ENDANGERED

the federal government was built to be impervious
to apology
as they weigh the extinction of species
against the economy of change.

their money is always on their money.

they are heartless, like the tin man,
but worse / because they don't want a heart.

a heart is weak and leads to love…

and love would fracture the story they've told
of their perfect past / in passive mood.

love would make them see
how they are as bound by the suffering
they set in stone to break the river's back

as I am / to a bullet in the gun,
aimed at a bird in flight.

ORDER OF MAGNITUDE

only my body knows the difference
between a wave and a bully wave.

a wave rises and falls
like the breath in my lungs
and pays me no mind.
it doesn't need me to notice its beauty,
which is what makes it beautiful.

a bully wave comes in the dark.
when my heart is bruised
and sits on my throat
until my hands and feet swell.

and I turn deep blue from wondering why
I must learn
everything there is to know
about myself
the hard way.

BANDED

I'm paraphrasing here, but…

something is wrong with me,
I suck at email.
I seem angry all the time.
I started talking back,
asking stupid questions.

I'm a crazy /dyke / bitch.

I should do myself a favor and not talk.

I don't understand the basic concepts.

I'm incorrigible and incapable
of checking a simple box…

I took everything
they said about me,
and I put my name on it,

and I sowed it to my skin
and wore it everywhere I went,
like I deserved it.

PEER REVIEW

if my people were here
they'd say / "fuck this,
let's go where eagles dare."

and we would,
and they'd take me home
to breathe the warm, dry, dreamy air

but I am peerless here…

perched ten stories above Portland
on a pink, plastic chair
in a late-night meeting with
my boss, a real queen-Cruella
and a three-star in the corner.

and we're talking about killing
fish-eating birds
for eating fish.

as if it made all the sense in the world.

DETERMINISTIC BEHAVIOR

my body makes up its own mind.
preferring to take the shape
of things I've been through,

sad eyes for the job
I should have quit years ago,

rounded belly for everything else...

FEATHERS

the edge of the earth is soundless.
solace for the length of January
that year-round residents,
like the dusky goose and I, endure.

I've lived without the sun
in rain, dark days,
mad dark days,
gone blood damp
in the howling wind
with heavy eyes.

with nothing to cover my skin
but the words I'd written
on scrap paper / taped together
stretched from shoulder to shoulder
blade to blade,
wing to tip

to remind me…

this is no place for heroes,
it is for people
in pieces.

SUMMARY JUDGMENT

after one whiskey,
I'll tell you I understand you.

after two,
I will mean it.

after three,
I will forget it.

but I'd still be more honest
then that big-shot judge
and his holy effing opinion
when he said it was legal
to kill / your kindred cormorants.

GOONEY BIRD

only a gooney bird like you
can teach us how
to lean indented wing
into that current of air,
that birds call home.

slip the mooring
of this hard, sheltered world

head high to the ridge
in the steeled, gray sky
above a tufted mass
of billowing clouds
rising over Baker Bay

only a gooney bird like you,

can call us home.

DEDICATION

I met her once in the low-light lobby of the Holiday Inn Express, near the southern footing of the Astoria-Megler Bridge. I was there for a public meeting on the Army Corps of Engineers' proposed plan to cull thousands of double-crested cormorants as part of their salmon recovery efforts. I recognized her from a picture I'd seen. She was crying. Her friends were trying to comfort her.

Nervously, I walked over and introduced myself. She recognized my name. I smiled awkwardly. "I hate this project," I blurted out. I didn't know what else to say. She looked at me with kind, bright eyes and said, "I have to go." She gave me her business card. I gave her an apology. As she walked away, I heard one of her friends say, "I'm so worried about Sharnelle. If they do this project, I don't think she'll get over it. I think it'll kill her."

After she left, I wandered outside to a path behind the hotel where the Columbia River meets the Pacific Ocean. When it had been wild, the river's main channel swept north near Baker Bay. Now it flows in a straight line to meet the preference of the Army Corps, who continue to dredge the river for navigation. That dredging and subsequent dumping of sand on nearby islands created ideal habitat for cormorants. East Sand Island, owned by the Army Corps, was home to the largest colony in North America, averaging over 12,000 nesting pairs. Years of research on their diet indicated they were consuming millions of threatened and endangered juvenile salmon and steelhead annually. To reduce this consumption, the Army Corps prepared a four-year plan to shoot the cormorants as they arrived in spring and then oil eggs in nests to prevent their hatching. Despite my personal and ethical objections, I was on the team that developed this plan.

Walking back inside, I spotted my boss talking to a reporter. Thankfully, I wasn't allowed to speak to the press that night. After years of working on the project, I could barely form sentences about it. It felt too stupid to talk about. A few days later, I read an article in the New York Times about the project, which quoted my boss saying, "This is a fascinating issue of how we as a society make choices about how we're going to use our resources for the benefit of one interest in society to the detriment of another," In my mind, I can still hear her afterthought, '...*and that's life, sweetheart; sorry if you don't like it.*'

Nobody likes the status of salmon and steelhead populations in the Columbia River, most of which are endangered due to the dams. The agencies tasked with their recovery are buried by decades of lawsuits and thousands of pages of binary thinking. In lieu of enforceable regional salmon recovery plans, a biological opinion (evaluating the impacts of operating the federal dams to anadromous species) functions as such. Full of assumptions and complicated math, it's a legal document used to support the government's conclusion that the operation of the dams won't jeopardize the continued existence of salmon and steelhead because after all the required mitigation is complete (like "reducing" the cormorant colony), they should be "trending towards recovery." It's a promise that is decades old.

I am not the kind of person who *trends towards recovery*. When I'm down, I stay down. And I was down the whole time I worked for the Army Corps. I lost myself trying to fit into their world and was too scared to leave it. When the official comment period for the plan ended, my job was to organize the thousands of comments received as either *substantive* or *non-substantive*. An email asking, "Do you have shit for brains?" is one example of a non-substantive comment. Sharnelle Fee, Founder of the North Coast Wildlife Center, wrote nearly thirty pages of substantive comments. All of which challenged the government's science and the assumptions they made in their reports. I read her letter in agreement but knew she could not stop the project. My only hope was that a federal judge would.

In March 2015, the Army Corps signed a Record of Decision to shoot the cormorants. Environmental groups filed a lawsuit and submitted a motion for immediate relief to stop the project. In May, the judge assigned to oversee salmon recovery cases denied it. He said the legal standard for *harm* to grant such a motion had not been met. The project began. Four months later, Sharnelle died.

On their journey from their natal streams to the Pacific Ocean, juvenile salmon and steelhead run into the Federal Columbia River Power System. Caught in eddies created by the river running into concrete and circling back on itself, they have what the Army Corps calls a *powerhouse encounter*. Some are swept up in water that goes through the spillways. Some are funneled into juvenile bypass systems put on barges or trucks to be taken downstream and dumped back into the river. Some pass through the turbines. Those who survive the dams suffer stress, trauma, and physical harm. An unquantifiable number experience *delayed mortality*, having been so injured that their overall fitness is reduced, and they die later in time. Like when someone's heart is broken, and they die from unresolvable grief.

The following year, I quit my job and moved to Astoria. I had plans to volunteer at Sharnelle's wildlife center, but guilt stood in my way – guilt for being a part of something that caused her suffering. I spent six years on the coast stuck in an eddy of personal grief, reflecting on the senselessness of the project, the bullies I worked for, the loss of my professional life, and wondering what I was going to do moving forward. I started writing about the experience, wanting to understand it.

This past winter, my neighbor invited me to dinner with another family down the street. During the evening, I mentioned I was getting a collection of poems published. I told them it was about the cormorant project on East Sand Island, and I was dedicating it to Sharnelle Fee. My neighbor, a well-regarded veterinarian, looked at me with surprise and said, "I met her when she first opened her center. I treated her injured birds." His eyes were soft thinking about her, "She was as good and loving as anyone I've ever met." He paused, and then a sadness washed over him, and he said, "I think that project killed her. She couldn't take the heartbreak of it." I sunk into my chair and felt like an asshole sitting at his table, wanting to be forgiven. Another neighbor mentioned she wrote Sharnelle's obituary for the Daily Astorian. She looked quizzically at me and asked, "Did you know her? Did you ever meet her?"

Acknowledgments

Thank you, Veronica, for loving me, fighting cancer, and waiting for me to wake up so I could be by your side when you died. Losing you taught me everything I needed to know about love, separation, and surrender. Sister, you were the water circling back on me when I wrote these poems.

Thank you, Livia, for loving me and supporting me. I love you.

Thank you, Nick Jaina, for your encouragement early on. I remember when you told me you thought these poems were going to be about a woman who went woo-woo at the beach after watching a cormorant. I wish...

Thank you to the Writers Guild of Astoria. Your support means everything to me.

Thank you to all the arrogant, pretentious bullies I worked with. I learned from you.

Thank you to all the kind and patient people I worked with. You helped me.

Versions of several poems in this collection previously appeared in Voice Catcher and Sixfold.

Nest Initiation - the phrase "an exact number of days" is borrowed from a Mattie Achord poem titled *Facelift*.

Peer Review - the phrase "where eagles dare" is taken from a Misfits song.

About the Author

Elisa Carlsen (she/they) grew up in Humboldt County, Nevada. She is an outsider poet, artist, and rusted metal fanatic whose work has appeared in *SixFold, VoiceCatcher, Anti-Heroin Chic, Nevada Arts Council,* and *Oranges Journal.* Elisa won the Lower Columbia Regional Poetry Contest 2021 and was a finalist for the Editor's Prize at Harbor Review 2023. Elisa is a poetry editor for New American Press. *Cormorant* is their first published poetry collection.

www.ingramcontent.com/pod-product-compliance
Lightning Source LLC
Chambersburg PA
CBHW031258120626
46545CB00007B/2882